CARRIE UNDERW...

PLAY ON ▶

PIANO • VOCAL • GUITAR

D0339564

www.carrieunderwood.fm ▶ www.carrieunderwoodofficial.com ▶ www.myspace.com/carrieunderwood

ALFRED

Produced by
Alfred Music Publishing Co., Inc.
P.O. Box 10003
Van Nuys, CA 91410-0003
alfred.com

 Contents printed on recycled paper.

ISBN-10: 0-7390-6268-9
ISBN-13: 978-0-7390-6268-5

Management: Simon Fuller, Ann Edelblute; 19 Management
A 19 Entertainment Production

Album Cover Design/Creative Direction: Scott McDaniel
Packaging Design: Tracy Baskette Fleaner
Album Notes/Creative Production: Judy Forde-Blair
Imaging Production: Tammie Harris Cleek

A&R Direction: Renée Bell, Iain Pirie
Photography: Matthew Rolston
Hair: Robert Vetica
Makeup: Francesca Tolot
Stylist: Julie Matos
© 2009 Sony Music Entertainment

CONTENTS

COWBOY CASANOVA

Gtr. tuned down a whole step:
⑥ = D ③ = F
⑤ = G ② = A
④ = C ① = D

Words and Music by
CARRIE UNDERWOOD, MIKE ELIZONDO
and BRETT JAMES

Moderate country rock shuffle ♩ = 120

Lyrics:
Oh. Oh. Oh.

1. You bet-ter take it from me.

Verse:
me. That boy is like a dis-ease.
face. You ain't hear-ing what I say.

Cowboy Casanova - 7 - 1
33489

*Play cue notes and chords in parentheses 2nd time.

Bridge:

You bet-ter run for your life.

Run, run a-way___ don't let him mess with your mind.

He'll tell you an-y-thing you wan-na hear. He'll break your heart.

QUITTER

Words and Music by
MAX MARTIN, SHELLBACK
and SAVAN KOTECHA

MAMA'S SONG

Words and Music by
CARRIE UNDERWOOD, KARA DIOGUARDI,
MARTI FREDERIKSEN and LUKE LAIRD

me.

Don't you wor - ry a - bout

me.

And when I watch

Bridge:

my ba - by grow_ up, I'll on-ly want_ what's_ best for_ her. And I hope_

she'll find the an-swer to_ my_ prayers._ And that_ she'll_ say... He is_

Chorus:

CHANGE

Words and Music by
KATRINA ELAM, JOSH KEAR
and CHRIS TOMPKINS

1. What-cha gon-na do with the thir-ty-six cents stick-y with Coke on your floor-board. When a
(2.) what-cha gon-na do when you're watch-ing T V and an ad comes on yeah you know the kind.

wom-an on the street is hud-dled in the cold on a side-walk vent, trying to keep warm._ Do you
Flash-ing up pic-tures of a child_ in___ need. For a dime a day you could save a life.___ Do you

call her o - ver, hand_ her the change,_ ask___ her sto - ry, ask___ her her name?_ Or
call the num - ber, reach_ out a hand,_ or do you change the chan - nel, call_ it a scam?_ Or

do you tell your-self...____

do you tell your-self...

Chorus:

You're just a fool,_ just a fool to be-lieve you can change_ the world.____
You're just a fool,_ just a fool to be-lieve you can change_ the world._ Don't lis-ten to 'em when they_ say_

UNDO IT

Words and Music by
CARRIE UNDERWOOD, KARA DIOGUARDI,
MARTI FREDERIKSEN and LUKE LAIRD

Verse:

1. I should-'ve known by the way you passed me by, there was
2. Now your pho-tos don't have a pic-ture frame, and I

some-thing in your eyes and it was-n't right._
nev-er say your name and I nev-er will._

I should-'ve walked, but I nev-er had the chance. Ev-'ry-
And all your things, but well I threw them in the trash,_ and

Undo It - 5 - 1
33489

Bridge:

You want_ my fu - ture, you_ can't_ have_ it._____ (Ah._____

I'm still try - ing to e - rase you from_ my past.____ I need you gone_ so fast._

Chorus:

N.C.

You stole_ my hap - py. You made me cry. Took the lone - ly and took me for a ride, and I

wan-na uh - uh-uh - uh - uh-un-do it. You had_ my heart, now I want it back. I'm

SOMEDAY WHEN I STOP LOVING YOU

Words and Music by
HILLARY LINDSEY, STEVE McEWAN
and GORDIE SAMPSON

all our kids___ that we had-n't had_____ yet. One

for your grand-ma and one for mine._____ Said

we'd draw straws_ when it___ came time.

Chorus:

I'll move on ba-by just like_____ you,_____ when the

des-ert floods_ and the grass turns_ blue, when a

sail-ing ship_ don't need her_ moon._ It-'ll

break my heart_ but I'll_ get_ through, some-

day_ when I_ stop lov-ing you._

Someday When I Stop Loving You - 9 - 4
33489

39

Verse 3:

3. I bet____ all I had____ on a thing called____ love._____ I guess in the end____ it____ was-n't e - nough. And it's hard____ to watch____ you leave right____

42

SONGS LIKE THIS

Words and Music by
MARTY DODSON, JERRY FLOWERS
and TOM SHAPIRO

*Recorded in F# with guitar tuned down a half step.

**First time, piano part plays the figure from bars 1 and 2 from this point till measure 17. No chords through this section.

Songs Like This - 6 - 1
33489

Bridge:

songs___ like this one___ that tell___ the whole world___ just

what___ a jerk you___ are.___

TEMPORARY HOME

Words and Music by
CARRIE UNDERWOOD, LUKE LAIRD
and ZAC MALOY

Temporary Home - 6 - 1
33489

Chorus:

it's not where I be - long._____ Win - dows and rooms__
it's not where we be - long._____ Win - dows and rooms__

that I'm pass - ing through.__ This is just__ a stop__
that we're pass - ing through.__ This is just__ a stop__

on the way to where_ I'm go - ing.____ I'm not a - fraid__
on the way to where_ we're go - ing.____ I'm not a - fraid__

be - cause__ I know_____ this is my__
be - cause__ I know_____ this is our__

THIS TIME

Words and Music by
HILLARY LINDSEY, STEVE McEWAN
and GORDIE SAMPSON

Chorus:

Maybe it's the way that the night is still, ___ or the sound of the rain on my window sill, ___ yeah, ___ yeah.

LOOK AT ME

Words and Music by
JIM COLLINS and PAUL OVERSTREET

like I've_____ done_____ be - fore.   Dar - ling

what I've been wait - ing_____ to_____ find._____ Dar - ling

Chorus:

look_____ at   me._____   I've fall - en like a   fool   for   you.__

_____   Dar - ling   can't_____ you_____   see._____   I'd do an - y - thing you

UNAPOLOGIZE

Words and Music by
CARRIE UNDERWOOD, HILLARY LINDSEY,
RAINE MAIDA and CHANTAL KREVIAZUK

Moderately slow ♩ = 84

Unapologize - 8 - 1
33489

Chorus:

WHAT CAN I SAY

Words and Music by
CARRIE UNDERWOOD, DAVID HODGES
and STEVE McEWAN

Verse 1:

eyes are red,__ watched your tail - lights in the rain.__ Emp - ty heart__

filled with re - gret,__ I know we__ were both__ to blame.__ And I'm not

Female:

1. Pierc - ing words,__

What Can I Say - 8 - 1
33489

up the phone_ a thou - sand times_ and tried to dial_____ your num - ber. But it's been_____

_ so long._____ It's nev - er eas - y.____ It's like

tryin' to spin_ the world____ the oth - er way.____ What can I___

_ say?_____ **Male:** 2. How did it___

(with pedal)

Chorus:

PLAY ON

Words and Music by
CARRIE UNDERWOOD, NATALIE HEMBY
and LUKE LAIRD

Moderately ♩ = 92

Play On - 7 - 1
33489